The go-

Here comes
the red go-kart.

Here comes

the orange go-kart.

Here comes

the yellow go-kart.

Here comes

the green go-kart.

Here comes

the blue go-kart.

Here comes

the purple go-kart.

Here comes

the white go-kart.

Here comes the winner!